LOVING MY LORD
Through Poetry

Psalm 34:3 Barbara Speicher

BARBARA SPEICHER

WESTBOW
PRESS®
A DIVISION OF THOMAS NELSON
& ZONDERVAN

Copyright © 2017 Barbara Speicher.

All rights reserved. No part of this book may be used or reproduced by any means, graphic, electronic, or mechanical, including photocopying, recording, taping or by any information storage retrieval system without the written permission of the author except in the case of brief quotations embodied in critical articles and reviews.

Scripture quotations marked NASB are taken from the New American Standard Bible, Copyright 1960, 1962, 1963, 1968, 1971, 1972, 1973, 1975, 1977, 1995 by The Lockman Foundation. Used by permission.

Scripture quotations marked NIV are taken from the Holy Bible, New International Version. NIV. Copyright 1973, 1978, 1984 by International Bible Society. Used by permission of Zondervan. All rights reserved.

Unless otherwise indicated, all scripture quotations are from The Holy Bible, English Standard Version (ESV). Copyright 2001 by Crossway Bibles, a division of Good News Publishers. Used by permission. All rights reserved.

Scripture quotations marked TLB are taken from The Living Bible copyright 1971. Used by permission of Tyndale House Publishers, Inc., Carol Stream, Illinois 60188. All rights reserved.

WestBow Press books may be ordered through booksellers or by contacting:

WestBow Press
A Division of Thomas Nelson & Zondervan
1663 Liberty Drive
Bloomington, IN 47403
www.westbowpress.com
1 (866) 928-1240

Because of the dynamic nature of the Internet, any web addresses or links contained in this book may have changed since publication and may no longer be valid. The views expressed in this work are solely those of the author and do not necessarily reflect the views of the publisher, and the publisher hereby disclaims any responsibility for them.

Any people depicted in stock imagery provided by Thinkstock are models, and such images are being used for illustrative purposes only.
Certain stock imagery © Thinkstock.

ISBN: 978-1-5127-7470-2 (sc)
ISBN: 978-1-5127-7469-6 (e)

Library of Congress Control Number: 2017901831

Print information available on the last page.

WestBow Press rev. date: 04/19/2017

**These poems are dedicated to
my Lord and Savior, Jesus Christ.
I can't thank and praise Him enough!**

"He has called me out of darkness into His marvelous light,
so that I may proclaim the excellencies of Him."
1 Peter 2:9 (NASB)

Contents

Introduction xi

Jesus 1
    God's Gift 2
    In Jesus 3
    My Father Sent Me 4
    Jesus… 5
    King of Kings 6

Salvation through Christ 7
    A Simple Plan 8
    Salvation, a Free Gift 9
    Your Washing Day 10

God's Grace 11
    Grace Found Me First 12
    God's Well of Grace 13
    Wrapped in a Robe 14

God's Mercy 15
    The Lord's Mercy 16
    Unfailing Mercy 17
    Protected by Your Mercy 18

God's Forgiveness 19
    Seek Me Always 20
    Ruler of My Heart 21
    Forever Forgiven 22

The Holy Spirit 23
    How Can We Know 24
    Christ in You, Christ in Me 25
    Flooding of the Holy Spirit 26
    Just You in Me, Lord 27
    Your Son in Me 28

The Cross 29
    Not Just a Cross 30
    The Cross 31
    The Crossroad 32

God's Faithfulness 35
    Truths About God 36
    God's Glory 37
    God Marches On 38
    I'm Filled With God 39
    God's Unchanging Promises 40

God's Love 41
    The Greatest Gift 42
    It's All About Love 43
    I'll Put on Love 44

God's Word 45
    Your Word, Lord 46
    Use God's Word 47
    Your Word, a Treasure 48

God's Protection and Peace 49
    God is With Me 50
    God is Alive 51
    The Nearness of God 52
    Whether 53
    God's Perfect Peace 54

Valuable to God 55
    You Are… 56
    I Love you, My Child 57
    In Me You Are Complete 58

A Changed Life through Christ 59
    Wretchedness to Righteousness 60
    My Life, Lord, Did Change 61
    With God I'm a New Person 62
    A Clean Vessel 63
    Lord, It's You 64

Living for God 65
    God Will Guide 66
    Give 67
    Stronger Than the Enemy 68
    Take Your Thoughts Captive 69
    Lord, Thank You for Loving Me 70
    Lord, Let Me Be 71
    Like You, Lord 72

Praising and Thanking God 73
    You Are So Beautiful 74
    Praise Takes Flight 75
    Morning Songs 76
    A New Day 77
    I Must Sing 78
    All My Springs of Joy 79
    I Want Your Praise 80
    Giving Thanks 81
    Make My Life an Alleluia 82
    Never Enough 83
    When You Look at Me, Lord 84

Bible Translations 85

Introduction

How did all this poetry writing get started? I'm really not sure. I do know that after I accepted Christ as my personal Savior when I was thirty-five, I couldn't seem to read enough of His Word. I can remember waking up early every morning when I was teaching, 5:20 a.m. to be exact, grabbing a cup of tea, and heading to my office. It was my quiet time before the noise and activities of the day began, when I could work on my Bible study and pray. There was so much in the Bible that I wanted to remember. How could I make it more personal and also embed it in my mind and heart?

I found myself jotting down important phrases and creating word pictures that would help me capture the essence of the verses. I had no preconceived idea of what these thoughts would become, but they always seemed to eventuate into a poem.

I'm not sure why, but in this process of personalizing scripture through poetry, it became automatic for me to make them rhyme, for the most part. It got to the point that sometimes I would go to bed or wake up thinking of how to arrange words to create just the right verse endings. I can even remember driving in the car with a piece of paper and pen beside me to write down something that came to mind when I stopped at a traffic light. Since most of my poems rhyme, they can easily be turned into songs, and I've done that with a number of them.

Over the years, these poems and songs have filled notebooks. I guess you could say my writing is almost an obsession! Taking God's Word, digesting it, and then reformulating it into something that is meaningful to me—not only do I find that compelling, but it makes me feel complete. It's become a way of worship, saturating myself in God's beautiful mind. I am abiding in His Word and I love it! I know that Jesus said if we do that, He will abide in us and we will bear much fruit (John 15:4), and I want that most of all.

Almost daily in my life, I have asked God to use me for His glory. I have been very driven to praise and thank Him through writing, and if it is His desire that I fulfill this calling in my life, I want to be obedient. It's been such a blessing to me, but is there purpose beyond what I can see or understand? The words the apostle Paul expresses in 2 Corinthians 4:7 have become my humble plea for my poetry: "Lord, You are the eternal Treasure that fills these creations of clay giving them life and meaning. Use them for Your purpose and glory."

This collection has been written over a span of twenty-five years. I have organized the poems topically for this book. I could write on and on and never be able to say enough to express my great love for my Savior. That is why I thought it apt to title the last poem "Never Enough." I can never praise and thank God enough for all He has done for me. To God be the glory forever and ever!

Jesus

"We have seen and testify that the Father has sent the Son to be the Savior of the world."

(1 John 4:14, NASB)

Luke 2:8-14; 23:33-34

"For the wages of sin is death, but the free gift of God is eternal life in Christ Jesus our Lord." *(*Romans 6:23, NASB)

GOD'S GIFT

God gazed proudly at His Son born that first Christmas Day
Watched Him sleep so peacefully in His manger of hay
Wrapped in swaddling clothes sweet baby Jesus gently slept
Mary hovered over Him, with love her promise kept

Reaching up, God saw His tiny hands search in the air
Sighing sadly for these hands a cross would someday bear
Faintly hearing His small cry that through the stillness grew
Grieved this voice would someday cry, "They know not what they do!"

God could feel the radiant glow that warmed this lowly stall
Knowing some cold, dark day Jesus would die for us all
God wept tears of sorrow for this little life begun
Sacrifice so great, He gave the world His precious Son

It would be the only way that man was sure to know
Of God's grace and mercy…how much He loves us so
Open up your heart, accept this gift God freely gives
Christmastime and always, you will know His Spirit lives

Colossians 1:15,19
Hebrews 1:3

"For in Him all the fullness of Deity dwells in bodily form."
(Colossians 2:9, NASB)

IN JESUS

In Jesus dwells all the fullness of God
In human form, God comes to earth
Jesus, the radiance of God's glory
Born in a manger, humblest birth

The exact likeness and image of God
Sinless, holy, pure, divine
Spotless lamb, so innocent, small
Able to save and redeem us all

Child of mercy, beauty, and grace
Guarded by heavenly angels of light
Gift of salvation wrapped in God's promise
Our burdens lifted forever that night

God has reclaimed His precious possessions
Holding us close, not to lose us again
Giving His Son, God gained the whole world
All *we* must do is believe in Him…

In Jesus

John 5:19,30; 6:39; 8:19,28-29
14:9-11; 17:21; 20:21

"I can do nothing on my own initiative…" (John 5:30a, NASB)

MY FATHER SENT ME

(Jesus repeatedly said that everything He said and did
was directed by God; they were One!)

My Father sent Me; from Him, I came forth
My Father sent Me to accomplish His work
I see what He's doing; He shows Me all things
I do in like manner; He's in everything

On My own, I can do nothing; I live
by the commandments My Father gives
Coming from Him, only doing His will
What He desires is what I fulfill

Teaching My own thoughts is not what I seek
Only what *He* teaches Me do I speak
If you know Me, you'll know My Father, too
Seeing Me, you'll see all *He* would do

He who sent Me never leaves Me alone
I honor Him and make *His* glory known
Doing My Father's will is why I came
That I lose no one; raise them the last day

I'm in My Father; My Father's in Me
We'll be in you, if you simply believe
Peace be with you and in all that you do
My Father sent *Me;* now I'm sending *you*

Malachi 4:2 (TLB)
Luke 1:78 (NASB)
John 8:12 (NASB)
2 Peter 1:19 (TLB)
Revelation 22:16 (NASB)

"'While you have the Light, believe in the Light, so that you may become sons of Light." These things Jesus spoke..."
(John 12:36, NASB)

JESUS...

"The Sunrise from on high," heaven's dawn, breaking upon
all who sit in the shadow of death
and the darkness of sin.

Jesus...
"The bright Morning Star," glorious light,
waking the dormant, dissolving despair,
laying aside the deeds of the dark.

Jesus...
"The "Sun of Righteousness," shining forth goodness,
fallowing repentant hearts with forgiveness,
sowing the seed of new beginnings.

Jesus...
"The Light of the World," God's radiance,
revealing the barrier of burdening guilt.
"The Light of life," bringing to redeemed hearts
a harvest of blessings and hope.

Exodus 3:14
Philippians 2:10-11
Revelation 17:14; 19:5-6

"Ascribe to the Lord the glory due His name…"
(Psalm 29:2, NASB)

KING OF KINGS

King of Heaven, King of Glory
King of Kings, and Lord of Lords
Fullness of God in the body
First and last and evermore

Teacher, Prophet, Great Physician
Holy and Exalted Son
Intercessor and Redeemer
The "I Am," the "All in One"

Flowing source of love and goodness
Mighty, powerful, and strong
Grace and mercy beyond measure
Faithful Shield and Shepherd's Song

He's the Promise of the Ages
Word of Life, and God Within
He's "The Light," in Him no darkness
He's the Sacrifice for Sin

His name's higher than all others
All knees bow and tongues confess
Jesus Christ is Lord forever
Gateway to Eternal Rest

Salvation through Christ

"For God so loved the world,
that He gave His only begotten Son,
that whoever believes in Him
shall not perish, but have eternal life."

(John 3:16, NASB)

John 1:12
Romans 10:13
I John 1:9

"For salvation that comes from trusting Christ, which is what we preach, is already within easy reach of each of us; in fact, it is as near as our own hearts and mouths." (Romans 10:8, TLB)

A SIMPLE PLAN

God gave us such a simple plan
So everyone could understand
Confess Christ Jesus as your Lord
And you'll be saved forevermore

Believe that He forgives your sin
And sets you free from where you've been
Your past is not in front of you
Christ took it when He died for you

No need to read the Bible through
And understand all of it, too
You'll be no puppet on a string
Or helpless bird with broken wing
It's not a crutch for you to use
When you have nothing else to lose

Just humbly say, "God, I need You,
I pray You'll tell me what to do."
Then let your heart pour out to Him
And wait for answers to begin
Just how do I know that He'll care
Because I once was there

John 4:10
Romans 3:23-24; 8:32
2 Corinthians 9:15

"…for being saved is a gift; if a person could earn it by being good, then it wouldn't be free – but it is!"
(Romans 4:4b, TLB)

Salvation, a Free Gift

Salvation is a free gift from a generous Father
Given without question, with no strings attached
A gift of forgiveness, wrapped in tender mercy
A wonder that awaits to captivate both mind and heart

Reason tells me, in life, I won't get something for nothing
So God will accept me, I work hard at being "good"
On my own I find I cannot reach that perfect standard
My sinful nature keeps me from that coveted prize

All my searching leads to Christ who offers me a gift
Humbly down upon my knees, I take it as my own
Opening my heart, I find what I have always wanted
Fulfillment and joy, because I gave myself to Him

Now His Spirit's in me and to Him, I do belong
Brokenness made whole pieced together by His love
The simple message clear; it is not a mystery
Being saved is a gift that Christ gives us for free

Psalm 51:2,7
Isaiah 1:18-19
Jeremiah 2:22
Acts 22:16

"Wash yourselves, make yourselves clean; remove the evil of your deeds from My sight..." (Isaiah 1:16, NASB)

Your Washing Day

"Come, let's talk," the Lord does say.
"Let's make this a washing day.
Give me your deep stain of sin.
I can make you clean again.
White and fresh as fallen snow,
Your past sins will never show.
Loads of guilt and self and pride,
Emptied out with me inside."

You say you don't need God's help!
You can manage by yourself!
You work hard and scrub and fret,
Nothing works, the stains are set.
You are drained and all wrung out
With your self-helps all about.
Swishing, twisting, churning round,
Your head spins; no answers found.

Makes no difference what you do,
Smudges of your sins come through.
You see nothing will come clean
Unless it's on God you lean.
When admitting need of Him,
A complete wash does begin.
You can feel so clean and new.
God restores your life for you.

God's Grace

"For by grace you have been saved through faith;
and that not of yourselves, it is the gift of God;
not as a result of works, so that no one may boast."

(Ephesians 2:8-9, NASB)

Jeremiah 29:13
Matthew 18:12-14
Ephesians 2:8
I John 4:19

"God, who...called me through His grace, was please to reveal His Son in me..." (Galatians 1:15b-16a, NASB)

GRACE FOUND ME FIRST

Grace found me first
Grace came looking for me
It began in the throne room of God
A shepherd seeking lost sheep

Grace found me first
Grace came looking for me
It came from heaven through a baby born
So I'd meet God in human form

Grace found me first
Grace came looking for me
It is confirmed in a promise through time
If I would search for it, I would find

Grace found me first
Grace came looking for me
It is behind the gospel's intent
My righteousness at Christ's expense

Grace found me first
Grace came looking for me
It's all about love; God first loved me
All I must do is just believe

Grace found me first

Jeremiah 2:4-13; 3:12-15

"For my people have done two evil things: they have forsaken me, the Fountain of Life-giving Water; and they have built for themselves broken cisterns that can't hold water!"
(Jeremiah 2:13, TLB)

God's Well of Grace

In the dry desert of my heart
I stray away from my Lord
Thirsting for truth and fulfillment
Just a mirage I aim towards

Putting my faith in weak vessels
I build for myself each day
I find they do not hold water
I'm not saved by gods I've made

No pools that I pass refresh me
Or wash away my guilt stain
Admitting I am a sinner
Brings me back to God again

Fountain of Life-giving Water
My Lord's love flows on and on
A spring that spawns a new spirit
Power that lifts me along

From brokenness can come beauty
From dormant seeds new life grows
From desert sands hope can flourish
God's well of grace makes it so

Psalm 121:5-8
John 10:11,14-15
Ephesians 6:16

"I will rejoice greatly in the Lord. My soul will exult in my God for He has clothed me with garments of salvation. He has wrapped me with a robe of righteousness."
(Isaiah 61:10, NASB)

WRAPPED IN A ROBE

Wrapped in a robe of righteousness
A garment of God's grace
Cloaked in a clean white sinless coat
When Christ died in my place

Sheltered by a shield of faith
Secure from Satan's lies
I'm sustained by God's Word
'Neath His close watchful eyes

Bolstered by God's Spirit
Hedged in the power of prayer
Angels' wings a sanctuary
Protecting everywhere

I'm enveloped in a haven
Of God's love and peace
Tended by a Shepherd
Who, *my* soul, guards and keeps

God's Mercy

"But God, being rich in mercy,
because of His great love with which He loved us,
even when we were dead in our transgressions,
made us alive together with Christ…"

(Ephesians 2:4-5, NASB)

Psalm 103:10-12
Hebrews 10:17
2 Peter 3:9
1 John 4:10

"So far as east is from the west, so far has He removed our transgressions from us." (Psalm 103:12, NASB)

The Lord's Mercy

At any moment, God's ready to forgive
Wanting to wipe out all of our sin
Done for His sake and for our own
So never again will it be known

Treading transgressions under His foot
As far from west to east they're put
Casting them into the depths of the sea
"Remembering them no more," says He

Ready to forgive anyone who calls
Is Christ, Savior, Lord of All
Holding back judgement, so He can bless
All with a crown of righteousness

Wiping our slates perfectly clean
So nothing is standing in-between
Through Christ, God blots away our sin
He wants our lives to glorify Him

God's love is high as the heavens above
Full of compassion towards his beloved
What we deserved was paid by His Son
God is calling, "Believe Me! Come!"

Hosea 14
Ecclesiastes 1:14,17

"Stay away from idols! I am living and strong! I look after you and care for you. I am like the evergreen tree, yielding my fruit to you throughout the year. My mercies never fail."
(Hosea 14:8, TLB)

UNFAILING MERCY
(The book of Hosea is a picture of Israel's broken relationship with God: His warning, love, and redemption, meant for all).

God warned: You're married to a harlot each day
You focus on things and My love you betray
With no faith, kindness, or knowledge of Me
You lie and steal and commit adultery

Longing for idols has made you a fool
As you so haughtily break all my rules
Wine, women, song; that's the life that you keep
(What's sewn in the wind, a whirlwind is reaped)

You've broken my covenant, my love you've refused
You've forgotten your Maker and all of My truths
You've cultivated wickedness, a full crop of sins
Before it's too late, come back once again

Plead with Me, "Lord, take my grave sins from me
Be gracious, receive me, it's *You* that I need!"
You're not redeemed with perishable things
But by *My* grace, *My* love offering

I remain faithful, though you are faithless
I can't deny Myself, Lord of kindness
Bow down before Me and call out My name
I'm merciful always; through all time, the same

John 3:16
Titus 3:4-7

"But God demonstrates His own love toward us, in that while we were yet sinners, Christ died for us." (Romans 5:8, NASB)

Protected by Your Mercy

Protected by Your mercy, in Your sight beloved
Kept safe in Your Presence by Your redeeming love
The cross bridged the chasm, cleared away my sin
You reached out to save me, forgiving what I'd been

Lowly, undeserving, unworthy, and undone
You still loved me anyway and gave me Christ, Your Son
Precious sacrifice so great; the words I cannot find
To thank You for this act of grace that keeps us e'er entwined

Praise and hallelujah, joyously I sing
Humbly falling at your feet, my life, an offering
Always may I please You, evermore to be
A reflection of the love that You have given me

God's Forgiveness

"For You, Lord, are good, and ready to forgive,
and abundant in lovingkindness to all who call upon You."

(Psalm 86:5, NASB)

Isaiah 40:17,26: 59:2; 66:1-2
Amos 54:10-15

"For thus says the Lord to the house of Israel, "Seek Me that you may live!"' (Amos 5:4, NASB)

SEEK ME ALWAYS
(God speaks through the prophet Amos
to the House of Israel and in essence, to all of us.)

God asks: How can we walk together as one?
Your sins are between us, our closeness undone.
You go through the forms, all pretense and show,
Proud of yourself, your praises you crow.

Idle, indulgent, and all about self,
Not caring at all there are those who need help.
Rejoicing in how great *you* are in all things,
Your deeds, in *My* eyes, are less than nothing!

How you defy Me! Who made life begin?
Who formed the mountains and designed the wind?
Who called forth water from the ocean floor
To rain on the land, and made it pour?

Humble yourself! Repent! Come to Me!
Be good, do right, from all evil flee!
We'll walk together for *I* will forgive.
Seek Me always that you may live.

Psalm 139:23-24
Proverbs 23:26
John 14:27
Romans 12:2

"Let the peace of Christ rule in your hearts, to which indeed you were called in one body and be thankful."
(Colossians 3:15, NASB)

Ruler of My Heart

Lord, you know my heart so well
Sections broken lost, undone
Separated with no purpose
Now made whole by Christ, Your Son

Once my heart collected guilt
With my sins the tally ran
A dead weight; 'til I repented
And my freedom I began

Once my heart craved having things
More and more to fill the hole
Feeling empty, 'til You showed me
Serving self, a fruitless goal

Once my heart looked for excitement
Constant busy-ness (and stress)
Never hearing Your voice saying,
"Seek Me, you will find your rest."

Once my heart was proud and haughty
Self-importance was the game
Then Your light revealed a sinner
And Your Holy Spirit came

Lord, these sins residing in me
Kept me from You, far apart
Then I asked You for forgiveness
And You came to rule my heart

Isaiah 43:25
Jeremiah 29:11; 31:34
Romans 8:1
2 Corinthians 1:22

"If we confess our sins, He is faithful and just to forgive our sins and to cleanse us from all unrighteousness." (1 John 1:9, ESV)

Forever Forgiven
(What God would say to us when we believe)

Forever forgiven, forever forgotten
Your sins are not seen, precious one
Forever free, no faults, no guilt
You're holy and perfect because of My Son

Wrongs erased, not remembered again
We're one, no sins in-between
Christ's love covers you, you're a gift, My delight
My Presence is your guarantee

Forever your praise, forever your thanks
That's all I ask in return
Forever your love, being first in your life
Obeying My words you have learned

My Son paid a price bringing you back to Me
Make Him Lord of your life, Savior, King
He's faithful and true, with a purpose for you
Live for Him, be a sweet offering

The Holy Spirit

"I will ask the Father, and He will give you another Helper,
that He may be with you forever;
that is the Spirit of truth, whom the world cannot receive,
because it does not see Him or know Him,
but you know Him because He abides
with you and will be in you."

(John 14:16-17, NASB)

John 6:29
1 Corinthians 2:11-16
2 Corinthians 13:5

"And God has actually given us His Spirit (not the world's spirit) to tell us about the wonderful free gifts of grace and blessing that God has given us." (1 Corinthians 2:12, TLB)

How Can We Know

How can we know the thoughts of God
The mind of God or commune with Him
How can we move God's hands through prayer
Or of His Presence, be more aware

We can have part of God living is us
Helping us understand what we distrust
Showing us clearly what's right from what's wrong
Giving us power to stand and be strong

It takes one step to fall down at Christ's feet
Accept what He did on the cross and believe
Happening instantly, God's perfect plan
The work done by Christ to take sins of man

Beyond man's logic, we're baffled and floored
Thinking that *we* need to do something more
It's simple, we just need to trust in God's Son
Christ died for us; all the work's done

No sin between us, God views with new eyes
A place where His Spirit can come and reside
With obstacles gone, through a wide holy space
We can be blessed with God's love and grace

2 Corinthians 1:22, 2:14-15
Ephesians 1:13-14

"That is the mystery which has been hidden from the past ages and generations, but has now been manifested to His saints, to whom God willed to make known what is the riches of the glory of this mystery among the Gentiles, which is Christ in you, the hope of glory."
(Colossians 1:27, NASB)

CHRIST IN YOU, CHRIST IN ME

The secret is simply this, you see
Christ in you and Christ in me
Bringing the hope to everyone
Of all the glorious things to come

Christ in you and Christ in me
Christ in us, our guarantee
All our sins have been removed
And what God promised will come true

Christ in you and Christ in me
Wholesome fragrance God can breathe
A delight before His eyes
Because in us, His Son resides

Christ in you and Christ in me
Power for eternity
We have all with Christ inside
Now and always…fully alive

John 14:16-17
1 Corinthians 2:14-16
Ephesians 3:16

"But whoever drinks of the water that I will give him shall never thirst; but the water that I will give him will become in him a well of water springing up to eternal life."
(John 4:14, NASB)

FLOODING OF THE HOLY SPIRIT

Flooding of the Holy Spirit washing over me
Giving me the mind of Christ; how glorious can that be
Flooding of the Holy Spirit filling up my soul
Each time I surrender, relinquishing control

Flooding of the Holy Spirit drenching me complete
Seeping into every space, everywhere replete
Flooding of the Holy Spirit surging through my cells
I've been sanctified by grace, a place for God to dwell

Flooding of the Holy Spirit covering like the sea
Fruit of joy, springing up, for Christ's alive in me
Washing, filling, flooding
Holy Spirit come
Drenching, seeping, covering
May we be as one

1 Corinthians 11:1
Philippians 2:5
1 Peter 2:21

"The one who says he abides in Him ought himself to walk in the same manner as He walked." (1 John 2:6, NASB)

Just You in Me, Lord

Just You in me, Lord, let it be
Root out what displeases Thee
Anger, bitterness, resentment,
Unforgiveness, discontentment

Just You in me, Lord, in each cell,
In my veins and pulse as well
In my soul and in my heart,
In each living vital part

Alive with You, Lord, let it be
Fullness of Your love in me
Breathing your breath, with Your eyes
Both of our thoughts, side-by-side

Fill me with Your glorious power
Every moment, hour by hour
Empty me, wash me clean
That Your glory may be seen

Just You in me, Lord, let it be
Let Your life force flow through me
Reaching my hands; gentle, kind
Your love acted out in mine

Just as Christ surrendered all
To His death upon the cross
Humbly and in servitude
Not me, Lord…just You, just You

John 17:21,26
1 Peter 4:11

"By this all men will know that you are My disciples if you have love for one another." *(*John 13:35, NASB)

Your Son in Me

God, who do you see when you look at me
Do you see Your Son, Your precious Son
That's what I long for, and want to become
Like Your Son, Your beloved One

Do you see His arms in mine reaching forth
To a world that needs Your love much more
Do you see His eyes in mine that find
The good in others; to flaws are blind

Do you hear His voice in me, speaking truth
No matter what others might say or do
Do you find His heart beating one with mine
Desiring to be loving and kind

Do you see His feet and mine in step
Walking the Godly path You've set
May every move, breath, and sound
Prove that, in me, *Your* Son abounds

May Your forgiveness, love, and grace
Fill all of me, in every space
Help me to be like Your Son, precious Son
Our spirits united together as one

The Cross

"But God demonstrates His own love toward us, in that while we were yet sinners, Christ died for us."

(Romans 5:8, NASB)

1 Corinthians 1:18-31

"This so-called "foolish" plan of God is far wiser than the wisest plan of the wisest man, and God in his weakness - Christ dying on the cross – is far stronger than any man."
(1 Corinthians 1:25, TLB)

Not Just a Cross

Not just a cross that was made out of wood
Not just a man who was kind and good
Not just a story through history told
    of great men whose lives were brave and bold
Not just a book that sits on a shelf
    of parables, proverbs, and nuggets of wealth
Not just a people who praise and profess
    comforting words of happiness

That cross, important for all to see,
    symbol of God's love for you and me
God gave His Son, what a gift to bestow,
through His life, the Father, we'd know
Stories of people whose lives did depend
    on the love of God and the goodness He'd send
Book of prophesy, our Savior come,
    Christ the fulfillment, all searching done

The reason for worship and wanting to sing,
    He set our lives free; glad hearts do take wing
Soaring above all our worries and strife
    because we have Christ and eternal life

Luke 14:27
Galatians 6:14

"For if while we were enemies we were reconciled to God through the death of His Son, much more, having been reconciled, we shall be saved by His life."
(Roman 5:10, NASB)

The Cross

The cross reaches out from side-to-side
Like arms of God, opened wide.
Calling His children who've gone astray,
"My beloved, I've made a way."

The cross reaches up piercing the sky
Past earthly things to the throne room on high.
Grace of God stating, "I'll make you right
By my Son's loving sacrifice."

The cross reaches down bridging a span
From God, who is holy, to sinful man.
It is God saying, "I love you so much,"
And man responding, "I need righteousness."

The cross is a symbol, my burden is gone,
All to Christ, my sins laid upon.
He took my guilt and died for me.
Now God is pleading, "Just believe."

Beautiful cross, glorious plan
Perfect wisdom, God saves man.
The cross reminds us, *we* are His.
Christ in us proves that *He lives.*

Luke 5:31-32; 23:32-43; 24:46-48

The two criminals hanging at Christ's side were both sinners (like all of us), and yet, both responded to Christ in such a different way (once again, like all of us). These two individuals at Christ's death epitomize two varying reactions to Christ's call: repentance, humbleness, and trust, or the opposite: self-sufficiency, skepticism, and pride.

THE CROSSROAD

The crossroad of life for all mankind is
seen when Christ was crucified.
Jesus, our hope, on the middle cross,
surrounded by sinners, dying and lost.
The two criminals placed at His sides view
Him with such different eyes.

One is doubtful, stubborn, proud,
challenging Jesus right out loud,
"Prove You're God, and save Yourself,
then after that, save us as well!"
He tells God just what to do and might
believe, if that comes true.

The other man has lost his fight. His
heart is broken and contrite.
He knows that he deserves to die, and his
wrong deeds are not denied.
"Jesus," he most humbly pleas, "In Your
Kingdom, remember me."
On the cross, Jesus confides, "With me, you'll be in Paradise."

Which one of these two men are you?
Which one shows your attitude?
Self-seeking and confident, or realizing you must repent?
Everything on your own terms, or knowing
you have much to learn?
Putting yourself in first place, or seeking
the Lord's love and grace?

At this crossroad you must come. Life
or death, your choice is "one."

God's Faithfulness

"Now behold, today, I am going the way
of all the earth, and you know
in all your hearts and in all your soul that
not one word of all the good words
which the Lord your God spoke concerning you has failed;
all have been fulfilled for you, not one of them has failed."

(Joshua 23:14, NASB)

Deuteronomy 31:6
Psalm 139:16-18
Proverbs 16:9
Jeremiah 29:11
John 13:1, 15:3
Philippians 1:6

"The mind of man plans his way, but the Lord directs his steps." (Proverbs 16:9, NASB)

Truths About God

Truths I can count on
A storehouse of gold
Treasures forever
God gave me to hold
Promises I can believe every day
Now and forever
These truths never change:

God is good
He loves me, too
He's always with me
And sees what I'm going through
God cares about me
Each detail He knows
God planned out my life
He's in control

Job 38:8-11,25-27,33-36
Colossians 1:16-17

"Have you ever understood the expanse of the earth? Tell Me, if you know all this." (Job 38:18, NASB)

God's Glory

God laid the foundation of the earth
The frost of heaven, He gave it birth
He set earth's measurements, bottom to top
And bolted the doors where proud waves stop

He cleft a channel through desert sands
So floods could satisfy desolate lands
God is the Father of rain and snow
He knows which way the lightening goes

By His command each day dawns new
And He forms every drop of dew
God makes each tiny seed to sprout
And counts each one of our days out

The water jars of heaven, He tips
The rules of nature, He has fixed
God put His wisdom in our souls
Daily His power in nature unfolds

God's goodness is seen everywhere
Expressing the depth of His love and care
What is the purpose of all life, then?
To show God's glory, beginning to end

Deuteronomy 7:9 Proverbs 19:21
Isaiah 14:24,27; 43:13 Daniel 4:35
John 6:40; 15:5 Romans 9:11 2 Timothy 1:9

"Declaring the end from the beginning...saying, "My purpose will be established and I will accomplish all my good pleasure... truly I have spoken, truly I will bring it to pass – I have planned it, surely I will do it." (Isaiah 46:9-11, NASB)

GOD MARCHES ON

In every heart there are many plans
But God decides what finally stands
He's in control of what comes to pass
It's not *our* works, but *His* that last

Nothing that we ever say or do
Determines what God will carry through
He declares from beginning to end
"I accomplish what I intend!"

Why did God choose Moses to lead
Moses feared! It was his destiny
Why was Jacob put in first place
Did his twin deserve such disgrace

Why was Joseph the favored brother
God decided He wanted no other
Why was it Mary who bore God's Son
God said, "You are my chosen one."

Why was it Paul who heard God's call
He condemned Christians, worst sinner of all
Why did Christ die, an innocent lamb
God chose this way to save sinful man

God's plan for us has always been
Accepting His will and trusting in Him
He said, "Be in Me; I'll be in you."
Believe this promise; they *all* come true

Psalm 139:16-18
2 Corinthians 4:7
Ephesians 2:10

"For in Christ there is all of God in a human body, so you have everything when you have Christ, and you are filled with God through your union with Christ." (Colossians 2:9-10, TLB)

I'm Filled With God

I'm filled with God through my union with Christ
He gives me power, authority, might
His Spirit in me, alive in my soul
Is the same power as in days of old

Power so mighty beyond finite scope
It makes things happen when there is no hope
God made the world, His strength's in me, too
Ordaining my life, He'll carry me through

God knew me way back before my first breath
All of my days, in His Great Book, are kept
He thinks of me all the time, even more
Than all of the sands on all of the shores

God has a plan that He wisely unfolds
My life has purpose; He gave me a role
I'm filled with God and how will you know
The power and love of His Spirit will show

Psalm 89:34
Joshua 23:14
2 Peter 1:4

"I prayed to the Lord my God and confessed and said, 'Alas, O Lord, the great and awesome God, who keeps His covenant and lovingkindness for those who love Him and keep His commandments,'" (Daniel 9:4, NASB)

God's Unchanging Promises

God keeps His promises, forever unchanged
Everything He says remains the same
God promises He will meet all of our needs
He will give wisdom; He will give peace

God says He'll help us to overcome fear
When we're in danger, He's always near
Nothing can separate us from His love
No power below or in heaven above

Those who confess their sins, He'll forgive
He wants us with Him forever to live
His Holy Spirit assures we are sealed
And says "hidden things" will be revealed

God just asks for belief and trust
In the promises He's given us
So many lives validate they are true
By faith, you'll find, they are for you, too

God's Love

"In this is love, not that we loved God, but that He loved us
and sent His Son to be the propitiation for our sins.
Beloved, if God so loved us, we also ought to love one another."

(1 John 4:10-11, NASB)

1 Corinthians 13:1-3,8-13

"But now faith, hope, love, abide these three; but the greatest of these is love." (1 Corinthians 13:13, NASB)

The Greatest Gift

If I had a mighty faith well-grounded in the Truth
Believing I could speak and even make a mountain move
It would gain me nothing; what good would my faith be
With no love to show why God bestowed this gift on me

If I took all that I owned and gave it to the poor
If I prided myself on what I do for the Lord
What would I gain, in the end, doing all this "good"
If there wasn't love behind it, as God said it should

If I spoke all languages in heaven and on earth
If I had the gift of tongues as God's ambassador
I'd just be a clanging symbol or a noisy gong
If I did not show my love for others all along

If I knew everything - the future I could see
If God blessed me with the wondrous gift of prophesy
Knowing all God's mysteries would be a meaningless call
If God's love for others was not seen in me at all

If I taught and preached God's Word, surrendering my life
Even to the point of death, being burned alive
Nothing would I profit sacrificing for God's Son
Without love for others the main reason it was done

All the gifts of God will pass away some future day
Prophesy and tongues and knowledge will be done away
Now I see in part, but someday I'll see God above
And realize that the greatest gift remaining will be love

Romans 12:9-21, 13:8-10

"Do not be overcome by evil, but overcome evil with good."
(Romans 12:21, NASB)

IT'S ALL ABOUT LOVE

Love other people and don't just pretend
With brotherly affection, really love them
Delight in honoring all as you should
Hate what is wrong, stand up for what's good

In all your work, from laziness flee
And always serve God enthusiastically
Be glad for what God is planning for you
Be patient when troubled and prayerful, too

When you're mistreated, in kind, don't repay
But ask God to bless them and lead them *His* way
When others are happy, with joy be impelled
When others are sad, feel their sorrows as well

Do not act prideful, a big know-it-all
Never avenge yourself, leave that to God
You should not quarrel, let peace to be your guide
Others should see that you're honest inside

Overcome evil, do good continually
A servant and selfless, like Christ, you should be
Pursue loving kindness in thought and in deed
Love does no wrong…love's all that you need

Galatians 3:27
Ephesians 4:24
Colossians 3:9-14

"Beyond these things, put on love, which is the perfect bond of unity." (Colossians 3:14, NASB)

I'LL PUT ON LOVE

Waking up each morning, the first thing I'll do
Is put on love because God told me to
Forgetting all my worries as soon as I arise
Stepping out clothed in the image of Christ

I'll put on compassion, so I can better see
The needs of others, not thinking just of me
I'll put on a heart that's gentle and kind
God working in me, *His* will, not mine

I'll put on words that are humble and wise
Using God's Word, that's where wisdom lies
I'll put on thankfulness and songs of praise
Lifting up God's name, telling of His ways

I'll put on forgiveness that overlooks mistakes
Christ forgave me, He died for *my* sake
I'll put on everything God wants me to be
I can do all things for Christ lives in me

God's Word

"All Scripture is inspired by God and profitable for teaching, for reproof, for correction, for training in righteousness; so that the man of God may be adequately equipped for every good work."

(2 Timothy 3:16-17, NASB)

Psalm 119:54-56,105,111,126-128

"I long for your instructions more than I can tell."
(Psalm 119:20, TLB)

Your Word, Lord

Your Word is a necessary compass
In the rough and uncharted sea of human experience.
Your Word is a whisper of conscience
In the noisy inconsistency of worldly chaos.

Your Word is a constant companion
Closely walking a step ahead, eclipsing trepidation.
Your Word is a wise counselor
Giving life-altering advice to and through all ages.

Your Word is a dormant seed
Waiting to be activated by care and attention,
Opening up the potential for beauty.
Your Word is a soothing salve on the hurts and pains of life
Bringing solace, comfort, and hope.

Your Word is a river source, powerful and thirst-quenching,
Providing nourishment and opportunity
For new life and growth
Your Word is the sweet air I breathe
Bringing fresh insight, rejuvenation, and joy.

Your Word is everything wrapped up in One.
Thank you, Lord, for Your awesome Word!

Proverbs 8:1-11
Mark 12:30-31
1 Thessalonians 5:16-18

"My instruction is far more valuable than silver or gold."
Proverbs 8:10 (LB)

Use God's Word

Use God's Word as the compass for your life,
The starting point, home base, and the plumb-line.
How could one dispute God's wisdom and advice,
So wholesome and good, no deception or lies.
His words are perfect, plain, and clear
To anyone with half a mind and an open ear.
Nuggets of wisdom, more valuable than gold,
Far above rubies, these treasures unfold:

You should love your neighbor and give to the poor,
Forgive your enemy, God's Word – don't ignore.
Be kind and honest in everything you do.
Always rejoice, no matter what you're going through.
Do not let anger possess your soul.
Always be patient and have self-control.
Think of God and others more than yourself.
God knows what's best for your total health.

Can you hear the voice of wisdom calling out?
Standing at the city gates, at doors, she shouts,
"Listen, everyone, how foolish can you be?
Let me show you common sense, don't be so naïve.
Let me give you understanding, not found anywhere,
There is no instruction book that can compare.
God's wise words are good, right, and true,
Obey His commands, and He will honor you."

Psalms 119:11,129-131,171-174

"Your words are what sustain me; they are food to my hungry soul. They bring joy to my sorrowing heart and delight me." (Jeremiah 15:16, TLB)

Your Word, a Treasure

Your Word, a treasure I search for each day
From these deep riches, Your wisdom's conveyed
Your Word, gold nuggets of truth, not ignored
Cutting my conscience with a two-edged sword

Your Word, my sunshine, in full array
Your mercy unfolding, Your goodness displayed
Your Word, a lamplight for my path, a guide
Wherever You lead me, I know You'll provide

Your Word, a new song that I will compose
Bringing You honor; You'll write how it goes
Your Word, my joy: honey, sweet, pure
Delighting my soul with promises sure

God's Protection and Peace

"The name of the Lord is a strong tower;
The righteous run to it and are safe."

(Proverbs 18:10, NIV)

Isaiah 43:1-7
Psalm 42

"When you pass through the waters, I will be with you and through the rivers, they will not overflow you."
(Isaiah 43:2a, NASB)

God is With Me

When waves of this world knock me down
When life's strong cataracts heavily pound
When sinking sorrows flood my soul
And painful tides of suffering roll

When drifting away in a sea of doubt
When shattering storms within me mount
When winds of worry whip up fears
In my despair, God speaks, "I'm here."

My sadness streams out, "Save me, Lord!"
My desperate cries, He'll not ignore
My tears may drain me day and night
But I won't drown; He'll hold me tight

God tells me, "Rivers you pass through
Won't hurt you, child, I'll be with you."
Eroded banks may overflow
But He says, "I won't let you go."

God promises He'll always pour
His steadfast love on me some more
Through storms of life, I'll carry on
For God is with me all along

Psalm 18

"I called upon the Lord who is worthy to be praised, and I am saved from my enemies." (Psalm 18:3, NASB)

God is Alive

I cried to the Lord for help and He heard
It reached His ears, every tearful word
He bent down from heaven, came to my defense
Mounted on cherubim; His aid was sent

Swiftly He sped with wings of the wind
Concern and compassion all tucked within
His brilliant Presence broke through the clouds
With lightening and hail, mighty storms low and loud

He reached down and drew me up out of my trial
Like a mother would rescue her drowning child
The Lord held me steady, led me to a place
Where I would be safe and my fears I could face

Surefootedness, wide steps, He anchors my feet
So I will not slip and no harm will reach me
His right hand supports me, so I will not fall
In His great strength, I can scale any wall

My tower, my rock, and fort all in one
My shield of protection is His salvation
Praise God, my darkness has turned into light
I'm sure of one thing, I am safe in His might

Exodus 14:21-22
Psalm 61:1-4

"But as for me, the nearness of God is my good; I have made the Lord God my refuge, that I may tell of all Your works."
(Psalm 73:28, NASB)

The Nearness of God

My soul waits silently for God alone
He's my salvation, my solace, my home
Rock of my strength, a soft feather nest
A shelter with wings in which I find rest

Quenching my thirst in a dry, weary land
Through muddy waters, my Lord helps me stand
Weak and discouraged, I cling all the more
Finding a stronghold, His words that restore

Dependable is my great God, indeed,
Dividing the deep seas, delivering me
Nothing else matters, nor ever could
The nearness of God is my hope and my good

2 Corinthians 5:15
1 Thessalonians 5:9-10
Titus 2:11

"...whether we live or die, we are the Lord's."
(Romans 14:8b, NASB)

WHETHER

Whether I'm strong, whether I'm weak
Whether esteemed, whether disdained
Whether I'm rich, whether I'm poor
Salvation through Christ is mine to claim

Whether I'm well-known, whether I'm not
Whether imprisoned, whether I'm free
Whether I'm young, whether I'm old
My Savior, Jesus, died for me

Whether awake, whether asleep
Whether beginning, whether the end
Whether I'm here, whether I'm gone
I am the Lord's, my life, He'll defend

Philippians. 4:5-7
Matthew 11:28-30

"You will keep him in perfect peace whose mind is stayed on you, because he trusts in you." (Isaiah 26:3, ESV)

God's Perfect Peace

Do you want more of God's peace,
more of His love, more of His power?
If you really want to know God better,
you must let God have His way with you.
You must learn to have more faith,
put aside your own wants and desires,
look for ways to serve others,
and practice doing good.

You must trust that our good Lord works His will through you,
making you stronger with purpose and power.
If you put your life into His hands,
plead for His mercy, pay attention to His Word,
and pray much for others,
then God promises His perfect peace,
that passes all understanding,
will not depart from you.

Valuable to God

"…you are precious to me,
and honored, and I love you."

(Isaiah 43:4b, TLB)

Matthew 5:13-14
John 15:14
1 Corinthians 3:16; 12:27
2 Corinthians 3:2-3; 5:20
1 Peter 2:5,9

"For we are God's masterpiece. He has created us anew in Christ Jesus..." (Ephesians 2:10a, TLB)

You Are...

You are the salt and light of the earth
You are My body doing My work
You are My temple, a living stone
A household citizen of My own

You are My friend, co-worker, field
You are My child, who My Spirit sealed
You are My daughter, heir, and seed
A letter, ambassador, extension of Me

You are my chosen one, "called," and strong
You are a branch My promise lives on
You're My beloved, created to be
A beautiful masterpiece, precious indeed

Romans 15:13
Ephesians 2:10; 3:17-19
Revelation 3:20

"…I have redeemed you; I have called you by name; you are Mine!" (Isaiah 43:1b, NASB)

I Love you, My Child

I love you, My child, for you are mine
You're a creation of unique design
I long to be close, so you will know
You are here to make *My* glory show

Even when you turn away, I still call
Your love is what I want most of all
Sorrowful tears fill my eyes when I see
My empty arms where you're meant to be

I've always loved you right from the start
I made you like Me, with soul and heart
I gave you free will to think and to choose
I want your trust, so no one I lose

All your possessions mean nothing, not one
When death is calling, and your life is done
Are earthly things and all that you do
Greater than eternal life I give you

Fill the void you keep searching for
With Me and my love, you'll need nothing more
I keep on calling, do you hear Me still
Believe Me, receive Me, just say, "I will!"

Proverbs 8:30-31
Ephesians 1:4; 2:10
Philippians 1:6

"For in him we live and move and are!" (Acts 17:28a, TLB)

IN ME YOU ARE COMPLETE
(What I imagine God would be saying to all of us)

You're the focus of My love, I want you pure and whole
Without Me, you're incomplete, rife with gaping holes
Only My limitless love can fill your empty heart
My designs for you have been glorious from the start

You are My masterpiece, My treasure, My delight
I want you to lean on Me each moment of your life
I am here for you, cling to Me, hear My voice
You are not My puppet; love's not love without a choice

The void you feel, I put it there; it's one you can't ignore
It's in Me you will find yourself and what you're living for
In *Me* you'll know that sense of peace, that certainty you seek
For I will set you free from sin, I want you near to Me

My holiness and healing will increase as you let go
Dwelling in my Presence, resting in My love, you'll grow
Together we'll go step by step, we'll
think the same thoughts, too
My purposes I'm working out in *all* things…and in you!

A Changed Life through Christ

"Therefore if anyone is in Christ, he is a new creature; the old things passed away; behold, new things have come."

(2 Corinthians 5:17, NASB)

Romans 7:15-25

"Wretched man that I am!! Who will set me free from this body of death?" (Romans 7:24, NASB)

WRETCHEDNESS TO RIGHTEOUSNESS

"Wretched man that I am" for sin dwells within
How I want to do good, but my flesh takes hold and wins
Who will set me free from death, a prisoner of the Law
Thanks to Jesus Christ, my Lord, my Savior, and my God

When He came into my heart and took the leading role
Every member of my body longed for His control
Now, instead of *self*, my mind is set on things above
Holy Spirit living in me: goodness, peace, and love

I no longer seek the pleasure that the world brings
I no longer am a slave to sin or fear death's sting
All I want to do is lift Christ's holy name on high
Wretchedness to righteousness when in my place, He died

On my own, the battle of my flesh was never won
I am free from Satan's hold because God gave His Son
I live for my Lord's delight, His purpose…glory be!
Praise God that my Master now is Christ and isn't me

1 John 1:5-7; 2:8-11

"...as we obey this commandment, to love one another, the darkness in our lives disappears and then new light of life in Christ shines in." (1 John 2:8b, TLB)

My Life, Lord, Did Change

My life, Lord, did change when I finally let you in
Knocking at my door, my ears were closed because of sin
Opening my life, your radiant light came bursting through
Walls were broken down that kept me far away from You

Standing in the middle was Christ calling out my name
I knew I belonged to Him, for nothing felt the same
Walking now along with Christ, my joy just overflows
"Loving one another" is the path I try to go

When the dark world presses in and pride veers me astray
With the light of life in me, I know I'll find my way
I will seek God's will with prayerful steps, not on my own
Glory of God shining, guiding me forever home

Romans 12

"Don't copy the behavior and customs of this world, but be a new and different person with a fresh newness in all you do and think."

(Romans 12:2, TLB)

WITH GOD I'M A NEW PERSON

With God, I've been made anew and view things differently
Satan's busy tearing down our lives, it's clear to see
Divisiveness, hopelessness, bitterness, and hate
Selfishness and pride, swallowed whole, the devil's bait
He loves to see relationships destroyed and fall apart
It gives him satisfaction breaking everybody's heart
Instilling unsure minds with lack of morals, worldly sin
Deceived by what is read and seen, the goal is "fitting in"
Anger, vengeance, that's the game, look out for number one
Evil reigns and powers of darkness thrill at what they've done

God gave me new eyes to see destruction going on
Knowing man is not the threat, but evil Satan spawns
God has given me the strength to do what's right and just
Learning that to win the battle, reliance on Him, a must:
Loving others and the truth, deploring what is wrong
Forgiving those who hurt me, God's mercy passed along
Being patient, praying always, helping those in need
Inviting people in my life, and with my kindness feed
Never paying evil back, not quarreling with anyone
Never being lazy for God's work is never done

I will not let evil get the upper hand with me
Being new and different is what God wants me to be

2 Timothy 2:20-26
Galatians 5:24
Colossians 3:5

"Therefore, if anyone cleanses himself from these things, he will be a vessel for honor, sanctified, useful to the Master, prepared for every good work." (2 Timothy 2:21, NASB)

A Clean Vessel

Restored vessel: scoured clean, spotless, purified
All the tarnish rubbed away, glistening to the eyes
Polished smooth, shining bright, ready to be used
Holiness, godliness, righteousness imbued

No more grumbling or complaining, quarrels set aside
No resentment, bitterness, thoughtlessness, or lies
No more gossiping or anger, jealousy or pride,
All laid bare, uncovered; not one I want to hide

Emptied out, humbled, *Lord*, make this temple Thine
Walk with me, fill me up with only what's divine
Give me peace and gentleness, goodness, self-control,
Patience, faith, joy, and love; pour that in my soul

Dig the well of Your Word deep in my heart and mind
So when others look at me, only *You* they find
How I long to see the beauty of Your life in me
Ready vessel used for You and for Your victory

Galatians 2:20
Romans 8:4-5; 14:17

"…be filled with the Holy Spirit," (Ephesians 5:18b, NASB)

Lord, It's You

Lord, it's You who've emptied me
Of pride and all uncertainty
I'm a vessel to be filled
As you move and I am still

Flowing through my veins and heart
Bringing life to wasted parts
Seeping through the desolate land
Of hopelessness and sinking sand

Sins awash upon the shore
Of Your forgiveness, I'm restored
Sparkling clean, sifted pure
Like the breakers: steady, sure

Once a lost and broken shell
Made a treasure by Your will
Recreated for one aim
Giving glory to Your name

God of mercy, God of grace
My life was not made to waste
Beauty all around to see
The most cherished: *You* in me

Living for God

"Now, Israel, what does the Lord your God require from you, but to fear the Lord your God, to walk in all His ways and love Him, and to serve the Lord your God with all your heart and with all your soul."

(Deuteronomy 10:12, NASB)

Psalm 16:11
Isaiah 30:21
Hebrews 3:7-11

"...God says, "I was very angry with them for their hearts were always looking somewhere else instead of up to Me, and they never found the paths I wanted them to follow.""
(Hebrews 3:10, NASB)

GOD WILL GUIDE

Our eyes on phones and T.V.,
Appearances, outward beauty,
Worldly things, what we can see
God cries, "Keep your eyes on *Me*!"

Jobs that keep us on the run
Pleasures making life so fun
Busy-ness that's never done
God begs, "Put faith in *My* Son!"

Self-helps that will make us new,
Solve our problems, find what's true,
Bring us wealth; feel better, too
God declares, *"I'll* get you through!"

Wandering in life's aimless ways
In life's deserts, we will stay
Empty, feeling dry inside
God pleads, "Walk *My* path, *I'll* guide!"

We must hear God's voice today
Not let our hearts turn away
We must put God in the lead
Saying, "*You* are all I need!"

Psalm 86:11-13
Hebrews 12:28

"Therefore, since we receive a Kingdom which cannot be shaken, let us show gratitude by which we may offer to God an acceptable service with reverence and awe."
(Hebrews 12:28, NASB)

GIVE

Give yourself back to the God who created you
All for His benefit and His delight
Give Him the tools that will further His kingdom
Your heart and your mind, *His* power and might

Give God each moment to breathe His intentions
Let His desires flow out from your soul
Follow the path He's made for your taking
May in His strength, you learn to let go

Give God the glory that He's so deserving
Each day surrender and ask, "Who am I
That He would love me, when I'm so unworthy
Coming to save me, so I wouldn't die?"

Give God your praises like nature unfolding
Open your ear to His Voice deep within
Leading you onward, in humble obedience
Joyful, for life given you without sin

Psalm 97:12
Philippians 4:8
Ephesians 6:11

"...greater is He who is in you than he who is in the world."
(1 John 4:4b, NASB)

STRONGER THAN THE ENEMY

Fix your thoughts on what's good, true, and right
Give God your praise, keep evil from sight
Think on what's lovely and pure all the time
Don't allow goodness to be undermined

Dwell on the fine points in everyone
Guard against letting good thoughts be undone
Think about all you can praise God for
Don't let the enemy open a door

Thank God for all things, keep praise in your mouth
Satan will do his best to snatch it out
He wants our worship; he'll interfere
Stirring up anger, our doubt, and fear

Bless the Lord always, resist Satan's wiles
Give him an inch, and he'll take a mile
Surrender to God lifting up praises due
Greater than the enemy is Christ in you

Psalm 112:7
Luke 6:37
1 Corinthians 13:7
Philippians 3:13-14
Colossians 2:4, 3:13

"...and we are taking every thought captive to the obedience of God." (2 Corinthians 10:5, NASB)

TAKE YOUR THOUGHTS CAPTIVE

Take your thoughts captive, do not let them stray
Make *Me* your focus, trust *Me* and obey
Do not fear bad news, don't worry, don't grieve
Safely I'll lead you, keep your eyes on Me

Don't judge or criticize...do not begin
Don't let resentment start, quickly forgive
Forget what's behind you, don't dwell on the past
Yield to My Presence and *My* joy that lasts

Don't be consumed with yourself all the time
Think more of others, keep *that* in your mind
Let go of problems, and all that is wrong
Think about good things, praise *Me* on and on

Strive to bear all things, and hope all things, too
Believe you can do all things, for it is true
Controlling your thoughts is a difficult task
I'm here to help you, you *just* need to ask

John 15:10-11
2 Corinthians 10:5
Philippians 4:8

"You will make known to me the path of life; In Your presence is fullness of joy; In Your right hand there are pleasures forever." (Psalm 16:11, NASB)

Lord, Thank You for Loving Me

Lord, there is so much to do and to be
A lifetime of loving You, You loving me
I want to glorify You all day long
Hoping my life counts, Your will carried on

Help me to dwell on the lovely and pure
And on *Your* truth that solely endures
Hearing Your wise words above the loud din
So what you've planned for me, I will walk in

Saying prayers often like breathing with ease
In any circumstance, to make You pleased
Not letting actions of others guide mine
Being aware You're in me all the time

Lord, help me have *Your* attitude
Make my eyes see past self, and just You
Give me compassion to see others' needs
Reaching through me, may You intercede

Thinking of what I have more than what's not
Realizing what I lack, I know *You've* got
Each day's a gift of Your generosity
Your love and goodness mean everything to me

Psalm 18:2
2 Corinthians 3:16-17; 4:8-9

"But we Christians have no veil over our faces; we can be mirrors that brightly reflect the glory of the Lord."
(2 Corinthians 3:18a, TLB)

Lord, Let Me Be

Lord, let me be the pure reflection of Your Holy Spirit
Let me see anew like the blind unveiled
Let my life shine with the brightness of Your glory
Let me hear Your precious words, a treasure unsealed

Let my sins be poured within You who died to sacrifice
So I would be reconciled back to God, once again
Let me stand true to the Word, Your mighty weapon I possess
To fight the onslaught of my fears
And overcome darkness and death

Let Your Spirit be my Guide, for powerless to carry on
And beaten down from every side
There You are, my fortress strong
Let me feel Your Presence near, Your Spirit, my guarantee
Of my future, joy of heaven, blessings forever for me

2 Corinthians 4:7; 3:18; 5:1-5

"You are a letter of Christ, cared for by us, written not with ink, but with the Spirit of the living God." (2 Corinthians 3:3, NASB)

LIKE YOU, LORD

I am an earthen vessel that stores
A valuable treasure from my Lord
Sparkling jewel of heavenly light
precious and pure, the Spirit of Christ

I am a letter read by men
Written by God, not ink or pen
Sealed with His Spirit in my heart
When delivered, I do my part

I'm a mirror that has been cleaned
When others view me, what is seen?
May the likeness of God shine forth
A clear image of the Lord

I'm a tent that sighs and groans
It is not my permanent home
God's prepared a place for me
Christ in me, His guarantee

Like You, Lord, to be transformed
So it's You who will show forth
Make me anything You choose
I am here for You to use

Yes, I am here for You to use

Praising and Thanking God

"I will bless the Lord at all times;
His praise shall continually be in my mouth.
My soul will make its boast in the Lord;
The humble will hear it and rejoice.
O magnify the Lord with me,
And let us exalt His name together."

(Psalms 34:1-3, NASB)

Psalm 28:7
John 15:5
Colossians 3:10-11

"You are my hiding place from every storm of life..."
(Psalm 32:7, TLB)

You Are So Beautiful

You are so beautiful, You I adore
You are so wonderful, my precious Lord
You are my strength, my hope, and my King
You are my all in all, my everything

You are my hiding place, my perfect peace
You, I want more and more, as I decrease
You are the treasure I seek everyday
You are more glorious than words can say

You are my Savior; my life, You defend
You're always with me, my faithful friend
You are my sovereign Lord, glory divine
You rule my life, and all that is mine

You are my mighty One, righteous and just
You never fail me, it's You that I trust
You lift my spirit with Your loving touch
My life is Yours, I love You so much

Psalm 148:1-6
Revelations 5:7

"Praise the Lord! Praise the Lord from the heavens; Praise Him in the heights!" (Psalm 148:1, NASB)

Praise Takes Flight

On outstretched wings my spirit soars
With boundless praise to You, Oh Lord
Not holding back, but lifting high
Your holy name; be glorified

"Hosanna!" like the angels sing
I adore You, blessed King
My impassioned, grateful song
Fills the sky, and then beyond

Praise takes flight, so You will hear
My hallelujahs loud and clear
Upward borne by love that lasts
Mortal things that cling, I pass

With Your Spirit, I will glide
Awestruck at the peaceful ride
Mounting hope before me lies
On Your promises, I'll rise

Psalm 143:8
Revelation 4:8; 19:6-7

"O satisfy us in the morning with Your lovingkindness that we may sing for joy and be glad all our days."
(Psalm 91:14, NASB)

Morning Songs

More than the birds sing, I raise morning songs
Steadfastly praising You, wakening the dawn
Humbly adoring, I'm down at Your feet
Lifting my praises; that's when I'm complete

Though words are broken and notes fall short
I know You hear my affection pour forth
Within Your presence, I just want to stay
Delighting in You, Lord; I'm wordless to say

Creating new songs with all of my soul
Honoring You with each word makes me whole
You are the breath giving life to my poems
Inspiring purpose for Your glory alone

Just like a wind chime, the beauty begins
When You move the strings and bring forth the wind
With rapturous praise, I want to give more
May You feel how much I love You, Lord

Like sands on the shore and stars in the sky
My praise be vast! My praise reach high!
Glorious hallelujahs, as angels would send
May all my praise songs, to You, never end

Psalms 57:8-10; 92:104; 104:33

"Arise my soul! Arise O harp and lyre! Let's greet the dawn with song." (Psalm 57:8, TLB)

A New Day

God, You've given me this day
To thank You for all You have made
The limitless sky, the land so green
And everything that's in-between

Seagulls soaring o'er the sea
Sunsets blazing brilliantly
Breath of life You've given me
The beauty of this world to see

Arise my soul! A new day dawns
Let's greet the morning with a song
Let's awake! This day embrace
Not designed for us to waste

Let's praise God for this glorious day
Another one He's carefully made
Yes, God has granted us more time
To see His majesty, divine

Psalm 105:2-3
Romans 11:36
Galatians 5:1

"My heart is steadfast, O God; I will sing, I will sing praises, even with my soul." (Psalm 108:1, NASB)

I Must Sing

Stand back, flesh! Away you troubles! I must sing! I must sing!
I must break through chains that hold me! I must sing! I must sing!
Christ has saved me! He has freed me! I can't hold my tongue!
Praise must rise to heights of heaven, or I'll be undone.

When I awake, my soul greets God with songs of gratitude.
Through the day, my notes thrill with creation's rainbow hues.
Then at night, like birds in flight, my praise soars up on wings.
Knowing that, from and through and to Him are all things.

May my music be a fragrance: frankincense, so sweet.
If I can't express my joy, then I'll not feel complete.
I must sing! I must sing! Let praises from me pour.
To my Lord be glory and be honor evermore.

Psalm 84:2
Romans 15:13
2 Corinthians 5:17

…"All my springs of joy are in You." (Psalm 87:7b, NASB)

All My Springs of Joy

All my springs of joy, Lord, are in You
Not in earthly things, or in fruitless things I do
Continually, they stream from just one powerful Source
Your river of grace, my soul vital force

All my springs of joy, Lord, are in You
Not from my old life, but one You gave anew
They flow with sparkling water, pure and cleansed of sin
Free from murky whirlpools I was trapped in

All my springs of joy, Lord, are in You
Rising up and pouring out to give You glory due
I'm at peace in calming pools of water, unperturbed
Because I'm buoyed by Your strength in this fallen world

All my springs of joy, Lord, are in You
Refreshing me as I soak in Your words of truth
Gushing up in praise, uncontained, spouting high
Because Your Spirit's deep well is in full supply

Psalms 98:4-6; 150
Isaiah 43:4
Jeremiah 32:17

"Let everything that has breath, praise the Lord. Praise the Lord!"
(Psalm 150:6, NASB)

I Want Your Praise
(God speaking to all of us)

Look at this world I created for you
Each detail perfected and carried through
The sea with its creatures, the crashing waves
The light of the sun and the warmth of its rays

The dazzling of stars, dotting dark skies
Each blazing sunset, each brilliant sunrise
Breath-taking snowy peaks crowning the earth
The miracle of every amazing birth

The uniqueness of every snowflake design
Each different thumbprint with its distinct lines
Eyes that all have their own special blink
People able to feel and to think

Not enough thanks, or grateful songs sung
Not enough prayers, or good works done
Not enough written, or thoughts begun
To honor Me and My precious Son

I'm pleased each time you glorify Me
It's always important, what I long to see
Your reverence brings joy to Me, always new
You're My beloved, I delight in you

Psalm 116:37
Philippians 4:8
1 Thessalonians 5:18
Hebrews 12:28; 13:5

"And we know that God causes all things to work together for good to those who love God, to those who are called according to His purpose." (Romans 8:28, NASB)

Giving Thanks

If I love God and follow His command
To give Him thanks in every circumstance
Everything will turn out as it should
God will cause all things to work together for good

Fixing my thoughts on what is good and right
Keeping God's kindness and faithfulness in sight
Blossoms of thanks will grow within my heart
Breaking the seeds of discouragement apart

I will offer up a sacrifice of praise
Fruit of my lips giving thanks to God's name
How beautiful are the words that flow forth
When a well of gratitude is their source

I choose thanks and I choose love
I choose joy…I know it's not enough
My Lord, Jesus, gave His life for me
Humble, grateful, may I ever be

Psalms 35:28; 47:6; 86:12-13

"I will extole the Lord at all times; His praise will always be on my lips." (Psalm 34:1, TLB)

MAKE MY LIFE AN ALLELUIA

Make my life an Alleluia,
All of me, from head to toe
You're so worthy of my praises
I exist to let You know

Make my life an Alleluia
In the "ups" and in the "downs"
You're so worthy of my praises
From my lips may it resound

Alleluia, Alleluia
Holy, holy, is Your name
Precious Savior and Redeemer
Evermore, Your glory reigns

Make my life an Alleluia
All my days and all my nights
You're so worthy of my praises
Thrilling Ears of highest heights

Make my life an Alleluia
With each word and every deed
You're so worthy of my praises
May You be glad You made me

Alleluia, Alleluia
Holy, holy, is Your name
Precious Savior and Redeemer
Evermore, Your glory reigns

Psalms 7:17; 69:30
2 Corinthians 9:15
Revelations 7:12

"I will give thanks to the Lord with all my heart; I will tell of all Your wonders." (Psalm 9:1, NASB)

Never Enough
(To my beloved Lord)

Never enough thoughts, Lord, never enough praise
Never enough moments, never enough days
Never enough thanks, nor gratitude
To convey just how much I love You

Never enough poetry, never enough rhymes
Never enough writings, never enough lines
Never enough melodies, never enough songs
Expressing my praise that goes on and on

Never enough rejoicing, never enough awe
Never enough gladness in You, Oh God
Never enough trusting and doing Your will
Or desiring that I be Spirit-filled

Never enough heart for the feelings inside
Never enough love to tell you just why
Never enough time through eternity
To give back to You all You've given me

"Long ago even before He made the world, God chose us to be His very own, through what Christ would do for us; He decided then to make us holy in His eyes, without a single fault – we who stand before Him covered with His love." (Ephesians 1:4, TLB)

When You Look at Me, Lord

Thank you, Lord, that when You look at
me, it is not *me* that You see.
You don't see a person riddled with sin,
a person with regrets, failures, and imperfections.
You don't see a person who has said the wrong things,
acted impatiently, or with stubbornness,
someone prideful, self-focused, seeking acceptance from others.
You don't see an unforgiving heart, bitter, or resentful.

When you look at me, all of that shame,
all of that blame, is covered,
not visible to Your all-seeing eye,
for I am dressed in the royal robe of righteousness
through the sacrifice of Your precious Son.
When You look at me, You don't see my sin,
but only recognize Your beloved Son
who took it all from me when I trusted Him.
In its place, You have filled me with the beauty and goodness
of His pure and holy Spirit.

Oh, Lord, I can't thank you enough
for sending Jesus to save me from myself.
He alone has made me righteous in Your sight.
What a great price He paid!
Now there are no barriers between us.
I can come to You freely, unhindered,
and peacefully dwell in Your presence now and eternally.
How I praise You, Lord! Thank You for
Your great mercy and grace.
I am humbled and awed by the wonder of Your amazing love.

Bible Translations

Scripture quotations used for these poems have been taken from the following Bible versions:

NASB – New American Standard Bible
Anaheim, CA: Foundation Press (1973)

NIV – New International Version
Colorado Springs, CO: International Bible Society (1973)

ESV – The Holy Bible: English Standard Version Bible
Wheaton, IL: Crossway (2001)

TLB – The Living Bible
Wheaton, IL: Tyndale House Publishers (1979)

CPSIA information can be obtained
at www.ICGtesting.com
Printed in the USA
FSOW01n1801040517
33898FS